A GLASS *of*

HOMEMADE LEMONADE

A Guide to Spirituality for the Over-Fifties

Patrick Coghlan

Published 2008 by
Veritas Publications
7/8 Lower Abbey Street
Dublin 1
Ireland

Email publications@veritas.ie
Website www.veritas.ie

ISBN 978-1-84730-081-2

Designed by Lir Mac Cárthaigh
Printed in Ireland by Betaprint, Dublin

In loving memory of my Aunty Vera

*With grateful thanks to Tracy for passing on a
word of encouragement from God*

Contents

Introduction

Born in the mid-nineteen fifties, as a teenager, I studied the new school computer with awe and wonder. 'Wow! What does it do?' we asked the maths teacher, excitedly. At great length, he explained how it worked and that, with careful programming, it could perform a variety of very basic, but repetitive calculations. Now the scope of modern PCs and laptops, together with the internet, is phenomenal. With ease, many types of business can be conducted from the home; and with the use of modern mobile phones ... well, suffice it to say that the mind boggles.

Even in my lifetime there have been many discoveries and inventions that have changed our lifestyles almost beyond recognition. So, bearing in mind the microchip and computers, supersonic flight, space travel and modern medical discoveries, what could be so special and life changing about a glass of homemade lemonade that deserves a book to be written about it? Read on to find out!

Before you get the wrong idea from the introductory poem that follows, this is not a *Christmas* book. However, having said that, Christmas does seem to be a good place to start. The poem refers to the 'unopened gift from God' – the gift of his Son, Jesus Christ. In this book, we are going to begin to unwrap that gift: to understand what the Christian life is all about, how it is relevant today, what it means to get to know Jesus and how that relationship affects all the other relationships that we will ever make. My hope is to emphasise the practical nature of the love, compassion and teaching of Jesus; to talk about building and repairing relationships on the basis of a personal relationship with Jesus; and to illustrate the nature of servanthood and what it means to be *salt* and *light* to a broken world.

What makes this book special is that it is written by an over-fifty with people of that age group in mind. Not that it's a different Christianity … just a different approach to looking at it. Don't forget, it's not just young people who are important to God!

Each chapter introduces the theme with a simulated newspaper *Wanted* advertisement. Included are short anecdotes, which, at the risk of sounding presumptuous, I would like to think of as real-life parables. We all have a wealth of personal experiences, especially as we get older. I believe that, when we are receptive, God can use many of these experiences to guide us and help our understanding of his will and purposes. Hopefully, reading this book will encourage such receptivity. Some more direct pointers to stimulate this ongoing journey of exploration are included in italics. Each chapter finishes with 'A guide to spirituality for the over-fifties': a summary of the main points of the chapter. At the end of the book is an appendix, with an entry for each chapter, contained in which are some questions that are very pertinent to modern society, related Bible passages and a guided prayer response – to be used if required and adapted to suit the individual.

A Glass of Homemade Lemonade is not a personal Bible study, but it does have a scriptural basis – the Sermon on the Mount, some of the Parables of Jesus, but primarily the Book of James.

The Unopened Gift

Christmas …
> *Fun-filled festivities for friends and families;*
> *church choirs carolling in the twinkling candlelight;*
> *garlands of glistening red and golden tinsel;*
> *cards from sometimes long-forgotten friends;*
> *unwrapping piles of generous gifts;*
> *fleeting aromas of festive food to come;*
> *pantomime and … 'It's behind you!'*
> *'Oh no it isn't!'*
> *But concealed amongst the transient trimmings:*
> *a gift – in simple wrappings lies;*
> *with no extravagance or luxury;*
> *a precious gift of peace, hope …*
> *and of love for us to share.*
> *To a damaged world – to you and me – his Son:*
> JESUS CHRIST!
> *To many, still …*
> *… the unopened gift from God.*

by Patrick Coghlan

WANTED
Servants:

All kinds of aptitudes and skills sought.

Will receive training and equipping for the job.

Must be willing, committed and obedient.

Should be prepared to work as part of a team.
Good reward for the right people.

Any age, race, colour, size or temperament.

Male or female.

No previous experience required.

CHAPTER I

Serving Others

Based on James 1:1 and Matthew 5:13-16

❡ I have worked in a variety of shops, during my life so far, including a Christian coffee shop. There used to be an old saying – 'the customer is always right'. Obviously, the customer is not always right but, to me, the phrase portrays a useful image of what it means to serve others. It involves respecting the person who is being served, demonstrating humility and generosity of spirit, and giving them the feeling of being valued. I will admit, however, that there were times when I felt annoyed and frustrated by customers, though I tried not to show it.

Explore your own experiences of serving and being served: in work situations; as a parent or child; as a carer or someone being cared for; and as a customer.

JAMES, FOLLOWING JESUS' example, refers to himself as a *servant* – serving God and Jesus Christ, in serving others. When we take up that calling to servanthood, we begin to understand something more of the nature and purposes of God. In this context, servanthood demands relationship with God and each other; it involves loving and being loved; and it revolves around things like commitment, selflessness and obedience.

Bearing in mind adopting the nature of a *servant*, we are told in the Sermon on the Mount that the Christian life of faith involves being *salt* and *light* to the world around. There is something very fundamental about the physical need for and use of salt and light, and that emphasises the fundamental relevance of the spiritual application of that teaching to all generations, including us today. As we try to put that teaching into practice, we begin to realise that we need to be empowered by someone or something far greater than ourselves. There is such a power available.

Salt

What are the qualities of salt? Salt adds flavour, it is a preservative and it can be very abrasive. Sharing the peace, joy and hope that a relationship with Jesus brings adds flavour to a world that is seeking real meaning. Setting a moral example to others by trying to live according to God's standards adds a preserving quality to a world in which standards are falling – even to the extent of amorality. And, at times, being prepared to stand up and be counted making a stand on certain important issues is the kind of abrasiveness that can bring about change for the better.

❡ I enjoy cooking, but rarely use recipes – I just throw everything in, but with a purpose! Following the guidance of a number of well-known TV cooks and chefs, I like to add lots of different but compatible flavours. Usually it turns out okay in the end, but no two dishes are ever quite the same. There is a real art in seasoning – the line is a fine one between just enough and too much. Although, I believe that salt is more noticeable by its absence than by the generosity of someone who is slightly heavy handed with it.

In the Sermon on the Mount Jesus refers to salt that has lost its qualities of saltiness as worthless, of no purpose. Maybe that is the key significance of this passage of Scripture for the twenty-first century Western world: sadly, the saltiness of Christian love, truth, hope and morality is often more noticeable by its *absence* in society.

Think about the current news headlines. Do any of them reflect a society lacking in love, truth, hope and morality?

LIGHT
What are the qualities of light? Light is so fundamental to life that without it and the resulting heat of the sun, physical life as we know it would not exist. We would also be stumbling around in darkness.

❦ I am always thankful for the remote controlled locking on my car: many a time, returning in the dark without a torch, I have been very thankful to be able to push that little button and see my car illuminated in the distance.

Spiritually speaking, it is all about being enlightened by the truth. Christianity also involves being light to the world: sharing that truth with others.

❦ I have worked with the elderly, in different capacities, for many years now. I recall being told for the first time, by an elderly lady, that the thing she missed most about getting older and being on her own was having a hug. Many since have agreed with that.

The truth of the matter is that, made in the image of God (Genesis 1:27), though marred by sin, we all have an intrinsic need to love and to be loved. This is inseparable from the concept of *servanthood* and of being *salt* and *light* to the world.

❦ I recall arriving at the bus stop, at the age of about fourteen, dressed up in my blue school blazer. I spotted a girl of a similar age waiting for the same bus. She and I had known each other only vaguely at junior school. Now our paths had crossed again – and she was looking very pretty! Feeling typically awkward and embarrassed, I said nothing, but just stood waiting for the eight o'clock bus.

'Maybe tomorrow, I'll say "Hello",' I thought to myself. Days turned into weeks, but eventually I built up the courage.

The deed done, I thought, 'Maybe tomorrow, I'll start a conversation.' Once again, days turned into weeks … and eventually the young lady went away to boarding school – I never saw her again.

Awkwardness, embarrassment, fear and lack of courage are all things that so often prevent us from fulfilling our calling from God and meeting our true potential in life – to *servanthood* and to being *salt* and *light* to the world.

Just as we need to look beyond ourselves for that empowering to take on the calling to *servanthood*, to be *courageous* and to be *salt* and *light*, we also need to look beyond ourselves for our source of morality, truth and love. A drown-ing man is reliant on grabbing hold of a rope, a life belt, a branch – something outside of himself that is secure or buoyant. Only then is he able to pull himself up out of the water to safety. The source of that morality, truth and love is the person of Jesus: 'Jesus answered, "I am the way and the truth and the life".' 'As the Father has loved me, so have I loved you. Now remain in my love.' (John 14:6a, 15:9)

The same Jesus who promises us power from God through the Holy Spirit, when we follow him: 'But you will receive power when the Holy Spirit comes on you.' (Acts 1:8a)

A guide to spirituality for the over-fifties

Follow Jesus' example by serving others:
- Receive God's love and pass it on.
- Improve the flavour and quality of the world by being *salt* and *light* to it.
- Live according to the truth.
- Take courage.
- Be filled with the power of the Holy Spirit.

WANTED
Volunteers:

Are you able to cope with challenging and sometimes difficult situations?

Can you remain positive and optimistic through suffering?

Do you have drive, focus, determination and perseverance?

Do you learn from your mistakes?

Do you love Jesus?

CHAPTER 2

Coping with Suffering

Based on James 1:2-18 and Matthew 7:12, 13-14

❡ I recall an occasion when I had just taken a funeral service. I was standing outside the Church door talking to people, in a mixture of drizzly rain and sunshine, when something or someone caused me to look up. Above us was the most wonderful rainbow. I was suddenly reminded of God's unfailing promises – our hope in even the most difficult of times.

IT IS SO easy to look back on our lives, particularly the more difficult times, and beat ourselves up, metaphorically: 'If only I had done things differently.' 'If only the timing had been different.' 'If only the circumstances had been different.' 'Why me?' 'If God is a God of love, why does he allow suffering, pain, sadness and other traumas?'

Sometimes we do make wrong choices. Sometimes we find ourselves in situations beyond our control – after all, we do live in a world that has been damaged by sin and is affected by powers of evil. God doesn't instigate suffering, but there are times when he allows us to go through difficult experiences. God's purposes are sometimes beyond our understanding.

James does make references to such experiences testing our faith and leading us forward towards spiritual maturity.

Think about ways in which you have dealt with difficult situations in the past.
Have they been positive times?
Were they times of growth or guidance?

Such maturity demands that we develop a different way of thinking. We need to be Christ-centred rather than self-centred and we need to begin to develop a more eternal view on life. God has a plan for our lives if we are willing to walk in it, depending on his strength and guidance. Part of that process is learning from the experiences that we go through in life – good and bad!

James challenges us as to where our focus lies. Do we think as society thinks – with its flawed ideas – or are we looking to God for his wisdom? What are our fundamental values in life? Are they based on the lasting values of God or the transient values of a materialistic society? God is the giver of good gifts, 'Every good and perfect gift is from above' (James 1:17a), and he longs to give his wisdom to those who ask in faith (James 1:5-6); a fresh start through faith in Jesus, as proclaimed in the good news (James 1:18); and the gift of the Holy Spirit, once again, to those who ask in faith.

I would not wish to belittle the reality and hardship of suffering, but when life is easy and comfortable, apathy and complacency can so easily arise. However, during difficult times we are challenged to develop qualities such as perseverance, determination and faith.

¶ The other day, I was riding my motor scooter, with my son riding pillion. It was damp and breezy though it had been dry when we set out. Then came the rain – in abundance! It wasn't the enjoyable, sun-soaked ride that we had both anticipated. Then, as I glanced to the right, I spotted a tractor pulling a plough across a large open field. The furrows of fresh, dark soil were long and straight, promising new opportunity. The seagulls followed the plough, eagerly looking for something to eat. It was a lovely scene which brightened my spirits. I thought about one of the wedding presents that my wife and I had received nearly twenty years previously – a chopping board with a picture of a horse-drawn plough on it, and an accompanying scrap of paper with the Bible reference Luke 9:62: 'Jesus replied, "No-one who puts his hand to the plough and looks back is fit for service in the kingdom of God".' I understand that the essence of ploughing is to keep your eyes fixed on a point in the distance and not look back. The chopping board was disposed of some years ago, after much use, but the memory of the scene and Bible verse still remains, and has been an inspiration and encouragement to me many times over the years.

God is looking for a people who are prepared to persevere in doing his work, despite the hardships and opposition we meet in a broken world (James 1:12). As we plough the furrow of living the Christian life of love and witness (being salt and light), we need to keep our eyes fixed on Jesus in faith and not look back in despair, with doubts.

Are you the kind of person who sticks at things or do you give up easily?

They say that every cloud has a silver lining. Without wanting to sound flippant, when we love and follow Jesus, God can and will bring good from even the most difficult situation: 'And we know that in all things God works for the good of those who love him…' (Romans 8:28a) Our understanding of God's eternal purposes is limited. At times we don't see the good in a situation because it is only revealed to us years later, in retrospect; and there are times when we don't see quite simply because we don't look.

It is the contrasting colours that bring out the picture on a canvass and promote the beauty of the sunset. Without the darker shades, there would be nothing to bring out the brighter highlights. Against the dark background of trials and suffering are highlighted things such as the faithfulness of God, the love of Jesus, the goodwill that does still exist in the world and the opportunity to be a witness and example to others. How we deal with the testing times in life is part of our witness to other people – being salt and light to those around us.

℣ After many years of village ministry, I am all too familiar with narrow country lanes, often with a lot of tight bends and unseen hazards, of which chipped windscreens and trying to pass oncoming vehicles are only two. Never having had a good sense of direction, I have struggled to navigate such routes. In general, travel in these situations has not always been easy.

In Matthew's gospel, Jesus likens the Christian life to such a journey and, let's face it, road surfaces and travel were probably even more tricky in Bible times! The essence of the passage in Matthew 7:13-14 is that in the gospels Jesus never promises that the Christian way of life will be an easy one; in fact, his own life on earth is an example of one saturated with opposition and suffering – but there are lasting rewards. Transient, often very superficial pleasures are exchanged for unimaginable joy, love, peace, hope and fulfilment, now and for eternity.

What kind of pleasures do you hold on to: those that last or those that are transient?

In Matthew 7:12, Jesus instructs us to do to others as we would like them to do to us. I would like to feel that in my most difficult times, there would be people around me to support and encourage, as there have been. Within that lies a lesson for us all – that we should make ourselves available to help others through their hard times. I recall fondly a wreath that was at my grandmother's funeral. On it was written the words: 'You gave me hope in my darkest hours.' What an amazing tribute to receive!

A guide to spirituality for the over-fifties

When things get tough:
- Remember God's unfailing promises.
- Be open to the good that God is able to bring out of difficult times.
- Seek God's wisdom.
- Follow Jesus with focus and perseverance.
- Do to others what you would like them to do to you.

WANTED

Good listeners:

Applicants must be willing to develop
and use their listening skills.

They should not be too eager to express their
opinions, except when appropriate.

The ability to listen well will be given
to those who really desire it.

CHAPTER 3

Listening and Doing

Based on James 1:19-27 and Matthew 5:17-20, 38-42

IN OUR MODERN society there seem to be degrees of listening. No modern high street, park or bus seems to be complete without someone wearing headphones for a personal hi-fi; wherever we go we see people wearing hands-free devices for mobile telephones; radios and TVs blare in the background in the car, at home, on building sites, in shops and in waiting rooms. We are surrounded by this thing they call 'background' noise. Surely that is a different level of listening to the person who goes and sits in a concert hall listening to an orchestra or a band perform.

The same can be the case when people speak to us. I recall occasions when I have been preoccupied with a task in hand and somebody has said something to me. After mumbling 'Yes' I realised that I hadn't got a clue what had been said. Also, there's that switching off half-way through, when someone answers a question *too* fully.

❦ When training as a Christian counsellor, I was shocked at how bad I was at really listening. It was quite an eye-opener. It is very difficult to give another person our complete attention: not to let our minds wander, not to interrupt, not to look at our watches, not to gaze out of the window and so on.

How highly do you rate yourself as a listener?
Even if you consider yourself to be a good listener to others,
how good are you at listening to God?

Good listening is not just listening to and taking in the words of another, but it is in our body language and eye contact as well. It also involves paying attention to the body language of the person who is speaking.

James tells us to be slow to speak, slow to anger, but quick to listen. He recognises that the average person is far more eager to talk than to listen; to boast rather than to congratulate and encourage; to pour out personal problems than to be there for someone else; to be full of opinions than to listen to those of other people. Then there are those angry outbursts, when it would be far more fruitful to listen than to say things that we will later on regret.

Our listening skills need honing: to listen to the needs and concerns of others as a way of encouraging; to listen to the wise words of others, to learn and be advised and, most importantly of all, to listen to what God has to say to us. Listening to God may mean hearing audible words from him; it may mean listening to God's words through other people; but it also means opening our hearts and minds to God speaking to us through situations, scripture and that feeling of something being right or wrong.

A response is required. There is no point in carefully listening to God unless we live accordingly. In his life on earth, Jesus explains the law of God and is our example. He highlights the positive qualities of it – after all, it is an expression of God's love, mercy and care for us. Jesus emphasises that the law is not a case of doing the bare minimum, but of constantly going the 'extra mile' (Matthew 5:41). It is not restrictive, but a free expression of our faith in Jesus; a demonstration of the resulting change of attitudes and motives.

A guide to spirituality for the over-fifties

Hone your listening skills:
- Pray about it.
- Think before you speak.
- Practise listening – to God and each other.
- Act on what God says to you.

WANTED

Imperfect people:

Have you made mistakes?

Are there times when you have failed to live up
to expectations?

Do you want to be loved and valued for
who you are?

Apply to Jesus.

CHAPTER 4

Failure

Based on James 2:1-13 and Luke 15:11-32

¶ As a teenager, I couldn't wait to learn to drive. I recall the morning of my seventeenth birthday when my father and I set out at 7.00 a.m. for my first drive on the road – I could even tell you the route we took. For the next five weeks and five days I drove and drove and drove – and then passed my test first time. To this day, I pride myself on this success.

One year earlier, I had failed most of my O level exams. Sadly, for most people, as with me, life is a mixture of successes and failures.

Do you have any regrets?
Are their times in your life when you have failed? If so, by whose standards?

THERE ARE DIFFERENT perspectives of failure, depending on what benchmark of success we use. Modern Western society's view of success appears to be things such as academic achievement, the gain of material wealth, maximisation of profits, fame and empire building, and even the superficial beauty of appearance. God's view of success, on the other hand, is based on things such as love, forgiveness, servanthood and obedience to his law. There are areas where these two perspectives clash terribly. James talks about the demonstration of favouritism as being failure to live according to God's direction to love each other. He emphasises that even the breaking of one single aspect of God's law constitutes failure. Then there are those missed opportunities; times when we fail to be the people we would like to be; and when we fail to be the people God would have us be.

When we have failed to reach that benchmark of success, there are many different ways in which others treat our failure. Peer pressure can be extremely unforgiving when we fail to meet society's expectations. Families can be quite hard on us when we fail to reach the goals that they want for us. And then there's ourselves: so often we are harder on ourselves for failing than anyone else. So often we say things like:

If only I …
I wish I had …
Things would have been so different if …
I can never forgive myself …

Do you feel loved and valued?

I think I can say with confidence that it is part of human nature to need to feel loved and valued. I guess that is part of what it means to be created in the image of God: the ability to love and the need to be loved. I recall two occasions whilst wearing my counselling hat when I felt particularly valued by clients.

❦ Let's call the first client 'George'. I'd been counselling George for some time when he arrived one morning carrying a small plastic airtight container. He opened it up: chocolate chip muffins. 'I've been doing some baking this week.' He held the cakes out to me: 'Would you like one?'

Let's call the second client Diana: Diana was a keen gardener. It was Easter time, and she'd been harvesting daffodils to sell. She took a bunch out of her bag and handed it to me: 'I had a spare bunch, so I brought it for you.'

A gift, a hug, a smile or a squeeze of the hand – tokens of people's gratitude; things that make us feel loved and valued.

It's one thing to feel loved and valued when things are going well, but what about the hard times and times of failure? What about those occasions in our lives when we feel that we have let God down and when maybe society has judged us harshly?

The story that Jesus tells about the lost son (Luke 15:11-32) is all about the love God has for us, even though we fail. Think about the ways in which some fathers might have responded to the son's request:

> 'Your mother and I have worked hard for forty years, building up the farm – through good and bad times – so that you and your brother would be able to take it on and run it together. I thought that was what you wanted.'

> 'We haven't done all this work so that you can squander the money away on women, alcohol and extravagant living.'

> 'One day you'll thank me for saying, "No".'

> 'I still can't believe that you could even ask me such a thing – you've always been a selfish child – I want! I want!'

And how they might have responded to the lost son's return:

> 'I told you so.'
> 'You're not welcome here anymore.'

But the love of the father in the story is an amazing kind of love. His love allows the space to make mistakes. It is a love that is dependable and supportive – no matter what. It is a love that is unconditional, forgiving and welcoming – despite his younger son's failure. Such is the love of God for each one of us. God can enable us to move on from those regrets and times of failure, through his Son Jesus.

Do you believe that God loves you that much? It's true!

In the parable, the father's love for his sons is unconditional and forgiving. He gives the younger son a second chance – a fresh start – but the older brother's love is not unconditional. He refuses to forgive his brother and refrains from joining in the party. Even though mankind is sometimes slow to forgive, God's arms are always open wide.

A guide to spirituality for the over-fifties

You can move on from failure:
- Society can be very unforgiving, unlike God, our loving Heavenly Father.
- God loves and values you.
- He offers forgiveness and a chance to make a fresh start to those who follow Jesus. And he goes on forgiving the shortcomings of those who say 'sorry'.

```
┌─────────────────────────────────────────┐
│                WANTED                    │
│           Evidence of faith:             │
│                                          │
│       Are you a follower of Jesus?       │
│                                          │
│   The twenty-first century world needs to│
│   see it demonstrated by good deeds.     │
└─────────────────────────────────────────┘
```

WANTED

Evidence of faith:

Are you a follower of Jesus?

The twenty-first century world needs to see it demonstrated by good deeds.

CHAPTER 5

Faith and Action

Based on James 2:14-26 and Matthew 6:1-4

Can you think of ways in which you are able to show the world that you are a Christian?

WHAT OTHER WORD comes to mind when I say 'Bacon'? 'Egg' maybe? Or maybe the words 'Fish and Chips'?

What about the word 'Salt'? If you're feeling theological, you might say 'Light'; otherwise you'll probably say 'Vinegar' or 'Pepper'.

Some things just seem to be destined to go together. On a more serious note, James tells us that a really inseparable pair are *faith* and *good works* (James 2:17).

Gamblers often talk about a race horse being *a certainty* to win. Entrepreneurs have been known to describe a new business venture as one that *cannot fail*. Matchmakers may describe a couple as *made for each other*. But all these things are based on speculation. A well-used phrase of this century and the last is: '*You've got to speculate to accumulate*'. The problem is that *speculation* so frequently fails to meet our expectations. However, the words of Scripture are from God – they are truth – and they will not let us down.

In James 2:14-17 the writer passes on to us an indisputable fact or truth: Christ-like love will demonstrate itself in positive selfless actions (see also 1 Corinthians 13:4-8). Therefore, when we commit our lives to following Jesus and are filled with his Holy Spirit and his love, then that love will find its natural expression in us as we are led to help, encourage and build up other people. This outworking of Jesus' love within us will be seen by others, by ever-increasing degrees, as our personal walk with Jesus becomes stronger and stronger. This active and often practical expression of love, demonstrated in our daily lifestyles, is the evidence of our faith in Jesus.

❦ When I worked as a horse-riding instructor, it was always my policy not to ask anyone to do anything that I couldn't do myself. Sooner or later, as a client was struggling with an exercise, the challenge would be offered to me: 'You do it!' At that point, I would don my riding hat and mount up, confidently.

I believe that society today is challenging those of us who proclaim to be Christians/followers of Jesus to prove it: 'Prove that you have faith in Jesus … and prove that the Christian faith has worth.'

The *evidence* of our faith and the *power* of our witness (being *salt* and *light* to the world) is in good works; but the basis of our faith and salvation is in Jesus' selfless act on the cross and his resurrection and in our personal relationship and walk with him.

❦ One of my aunts was a tremendous influence on me during my young years. She never shied away from talking to people about Jesus, and her wonderful demonstration of practical Christian love was always clear for all to see. I will never forget going to visit on the day that her dustbins were being emptied. The whole team from the refuse lorry sat in her kitchen drinking coffee. It was my aunt's regular practice in the winter months to have them in for coffee; and in the summer she would give them all 'a glass of homemade lemonade'. At her funeral, the minister referred to her as a 'signpost to Jesus' – she certainly was!

But when could a good work not be a good work?

'If you're going to do it with that attitude, I'd rather you didn't do it at all.' I wonder if that phrase is familiar to you: either one that you have used or one that was used about you as a child. I'm sure we have all known situations where someone has done something wrong and got caught for it. Suddenly, they are really sorry. Is their sorrow because they realise what they have done wrong or because they have been found out? In the Sermon on the Mount Jesus highlights that it is not just *what* we do that is important, but the motives with which we do it. A truly good work is a good, helpful and beneficial deed that has been done with a Christ-like motive of love and compassion.

What is your motivation for doing good deeds?
Is it a loving response to a need, or a way of looking good and winning favour with people?

Are we going about our good deeds in the right way – God's way – not boasting about the good deed we have performed; not wishing to call attention to ourselves; not wishing to take the credit away from God; and not wishing to lead to embarrassment of the person we have had the privilege of being able to help? Once again the question arises: Where is our focus – on the values of God or those of society?

Beware! If we do good deeds modestly and with the right motive, our reward is in heaven. If we do good deeds with a wrong motive, we have already had our reward.

A guide to spirituality for the over-fifties

Let people see the evidence of your faith in Jesus:
- Selfless actions.
- Right motives.
- Modesty.

WANTED

Positive words that
build up and encourage:

Are you critical in a destructive way?

Do you use words that hurt people?

Are you someone who loves to gossip?

Would you like to change?

Apply in prayer to God.

CHAPTER 6

The Power of the Tongue

James 3:1-12 and Matthew 5:21-25

❡ During my years working with horses, I soon became aware of the power of the bit and of the amount of damage that can be caused by using one that is too strong or by misuse of the correct one. It is a misconception that horses are ridden almost entirely by the reins – and hence the bit in its mouth. It is but one of the aids used by the rider along with the legs, back, seat and voice.

JAMES LIKENS THE tongue to a bit in a horse's mouth. The tongue has so much potential to cause harm: never under-estimate the power of words to discourage and destroy, and the tendency to over-use the voice.

❡ In my relatively early days of riding, I attended a stable-management course. I recall asking the yard manager about plaiting horse's manes. He turned around and sarcastically replied, 'You'll never go far enough with horses to need to know.' His comment was scathing and discouraging. As such, I was pleased to prove him wrong at a later date, by passing my professional exams to train horses and riders.

Thoughtless, unkind and over-critical words have so much destructive power over the recipient. If words of contempt and negative criticism are heard often, the listener will eventually begin to believe them. Matthew 5:21-25 highlights the harm that such words can cause, comparing their effect with physical abuse and even murder.

❦ I recall an elderly lady who I used to visit regularly – she never seemed to be able to say anything good about anyone. It became a very depressive exercise listening to her criticising her family, friends and the staff of the care home. I can't begin to imagine how they must have felt.

We sometimes joke in the Church about the use the phrase 'I say this in love' as an excuse to say the most scathing things about a fellow Christian – but it really does happen. What about those selfish or self-centred words? We all know people who only ever seem to talk about themselves, their families and the things that they have achieved. They barely seem to draw breath. If we manage to get a word in, they have no interest in what we have to say anyway. Then there are those careless words. Have you ever put your foot in it, said something inappropriate, and the more you try to talk your way out of it, the more you seem to dig yourself into a hole? Eventually a point is reached when you realise that nothing you can say will appease things.

❦ Many years ago, I recall uttering a careless word to a friend. I hadn't realised the implications of what I considered to be a throwaway remark. I apologised, but could not turn the clock back or put right the damage that had been caused.

Then there's gossip: the sharing of information about other people that is not ours to share – and probably not all completely true either.

Which categories of tongue misuse have you practised? Thoughtless, unkind and overcritical words; selfish or self-centred words; careless words; or simply gossip? James speaks about the incongruent nature of the tongue, when in one breath we praise God and then we go into attack mode with the next. His desire is that our tongues should be tamed and used in a manner appropriate to our faith in Jesus: controlled, truthful, encouraging etc. It is not within the scope of human nature to achieve such a result. However, what we cannot achieve in our own strength, God can through the power of the Holy Spirit – but prayer is needed. It is a joy to watch people's faces light up as we offer them words of gratitude, truth, encouragement and unconditional love and acceptance.

A guide to spirituality for the over-fifties

Be an encourager and a builder:
- Avoid using hurtful, over-critical and unkind words.
- Think carefully before allowing the words to come out.
- Be interested in what others have to say.
- Don't give others information that is not yours to pass on.
- Try to say something uplifting.

> **WANTED**
>
> **People who would like to be wise:**
>
> Anyone can apply.

CHAPTER 7

Seeking God's Wisdom

Based on James 3:13-18 and Matthew 7:7-12

FROM A STORY TELLER'S point of view, the story of Solomon's wisdom when confronted with two women fighting over a baby has to be one of the most exciting Old Testament stories to retell (1 Kings 3:16-28). The tension builds as the sword is about to drop – how can Solomon be so sure that the baby's real mother will stop the proceedings? Remember, the special gift that Solomon requested from God was wisdom (1 Kings 3:1-12). This incident truly illustrates God's wisdom taking over from human wisdom.

What is wisdom and where do we find it?

¶ I remember class tests vividly from my school days: 'Write your name on top and then list numbers 1 to 10 down the left-hand side.' After that, ten questions, with one- or two-word answers followed. The whole class would then exchange papers and mark each other's work. When the papers had been returned, the teacher would call out our names and we would say what mark we had achieved. One teacher always walked around the school carrying a brown paper package containing sheets of lined A5 paper – just in case. He would very carefully tear the sheets in half, lengthways … in order to save paper!

General knowledge is a funny thing, isn't it? After all, who would need to know the answer to the question, 'How many teeth does a crocodile have?' Sufficient to know that they have teeth – very sharp ones at that! There are bits of information that *are* very useful. However, I always look upon wisdom as being much more than just acquiring a good general knowledge. I see wisdom as including the ability to apply knowledge to life situations.

❡ In my experience of life I have come up against a variety of different strains of wisdom. I recall one elderly gentleman sitting me down and challenging me with the words, 'Let me tell you my philosophy of life.' Much later, when he had finished, he showed me to the door. My head was spinning.

James 3:13-18 highlights that these different strains of wisdom fall into two categories: human wisdom or God's wisdom (heavenly wisdom). The difference between them is contrasting and clear cut. Which source of wisdom we choose to live by will be obvious by the lifestyles we live. Heavenly wisdom is recognised in particular by the resulting quality of humility displayed in service to others. It comes out in God's values: unconditional love, compassion, generosity, forgiveness, selflessness, acceptance of others etc. These are all so clearly illustrated by the life of Jesus – our example.

❡ I'm sure that, at some time or another, we have all ended up buying something that we didn't intend to buy. Once we have been encouraged to buy what we need, the persuasive powers of advertising try to persuade us to buy what we don't need. Perhaps that is a reflection on modern Western society.

In the world around us, we can see the values that are attributed to human wisdom. Greed: selfish ambition, maximisation of profits at any cost, materialistic society. Power seeking: accepting a position of authority with the wrong motives, manipulating others in order to gain power etc. Vanity: yielding to the pressure of many of the glossy advertisements to try to defeat the ageing process. Prejudice: rejection of people who don't fit into the mould of 'normality' or who have a different coloured skin etc. The 'Me' culture – look after Number One.

Sadly, peer pressure and the influence of society are very strong in pulling us towards human wisdom and away from God's wisdom. So much so that we find ourselves in a constant battle. James describes human wisdom as unspiritual and, furthermore, attributes it to the devil. Such qualities provide a perfect opportunity for the devil to do his work and so the ripples of evil and havoc spread beyond our wildest imagination.

In verse 17, James lists the good qualities that arise from heavenly wisdom and describes it in terms of fruitfulness: 'But the wisdom that comes from heaven is first of all pure; then peace loving, considerate, submissive, full of mercy and good fruit, impartial and sincere.' He picks up this metaphor again in the last verse of this chapter as he speaks about a harvest. If we want to live in a world where God's values are paramount, then that is the seed that we have to sow – the seed of heavenly wisdom.

❡ When I was very young, I often used to go out with my Dad when he went preaching locally. Later on, I used to play one or two hymns on my recorder or piano accordion. Sometimes I had to listen to the same sermon on more than one occasion. It was during those early and influential years that I came to the realisation that God was calling me to a teaching ministry.

Who were the people that had a positive influence on you as you grew up?

I'm sure we can all think back to godly people we have known in our lives who have had a great influence on us – for good. Maybe they were instrumental to us entering the Christian faith; perhaps they were mentors to us in difficult times; or they could have been examples to us of living the Christian life. I thank God for people like that in my life, who helped me to appreciate the value of wisdom from God.

A guide to spirituality for the over-fifties

Seek wisdom from God:
- Prayerfully seek wisdom from God.
- Follow Jesus' example of humility in serving others.
- Live according to God's values.
- Do not be swayed by peer pressure.
- Sow the seed of heavenly wisdom in the world today.

WANTED

People with courage
and conviction:

Are you prepared to stand up for what is right?

Would you endure persecution for your faith?

Will you stand apart from the
crowd when it counts?

Help will be given to those who ask.

CHAPTER 8

Dealing with Peer Pressure

Based on James 4:1-17, Matthew 5:13-16 and Matthew 7:13-14

❡ I recall vividly growing up in the nineteen-sixties and seventies. My older brother and I, together with our peers at school, went through phases of listening to beat music, growing our hair long, wearing flared trousers, cowboy boots and flowered ties – among other things.

TODAY OUR YOUNG people are under pressure to wear particular brands of clothing. Worse than this, they are often pressured into things like taking drugs, alcohol abuse and crime. However, pressure to conform is not just something that affects young people.

In what ways do you conform to peer pressure?
In what ways do you refuse to go with the crowd?

There seems to be something about human nature that yearns for conformity. Even those who have claimed to be 'drop outs' over the years seem to have developed a conformity all of their own. On top of that we appear to have an intrinsic need for the approval of others. We don't like to be isolated. Having been on a number of different committees over the years, I recall various occasions when I was under the impression that I was speaking out for the majority, only to discover that I stood alone. It's a strange feeling!

James chapter four speaks about not conforming with the ways of the world, in other words not allowing ourselves to be dictated to by the falling standards that society often seems to set today. There is a subtle but very important division between being sufficiently involved in the world to *make a difference* for Jesus, and becoming indoctrinated by the ways and standards of the world in which we live. Many of those ways and standards are not of God.

When Jesus talks about the wide and narrow gates, he is warning us about the destructive power of going with the flow of pressure to conform. The devil works in many different guises as he applies pressure on us. Society, too frequently, is accepting of the falling standards of morality today. In some ways, the law of the land makes it increasingly difficult to make a stand against things with which we disagree. The advertising world, together with suppliers and retailers, appears to set trends in such a way that we so often feel obliged to conform. We don't want to be the odd one out, disappoint or lose credibility among work colleagues etc. Time after time, in the New Testament, Jesus sets us the example of looking to Scripture for the values on which we should base our lives – God's values – the same values that we see demonstrated in Jesus' life on earth.

Where do you look to for your example?
Who is looking at you to see what kind of example you are setting?

❡ A number of years ago, before cars were quite so well protected against corrosion, my Dad sold a car to one of my aunts. It was in immaculate condition. My aunt lived by the sea. It appeared that all too soon the effect of the salt in the sea air took its toll on the vehicle.

Abrasiveness can be very harmful in certain circumstances. We know, for example, not to use scourers on the best non-stick pans. However, there are occasions when the use of something with abrasive qualities can bring the best out in an object.

℣ My son and I love watching car programmes on the TV. It amazes me that, after applying paint to a vehicle, something abrasive appears to be used to rub it down to give the maximum sheen possible. Indeed, I understand that car polish has such abrasive qualities.

As followers of Jesus there are times when, in order to be *salt*, we need to be abrasive and stand alone for what we know to be right. Only that way can we be noticed – and counted – and hopefully have a positive effect.

Will you stand alone when it is necessary?

Jesus likens the Christian journey to travelling on a narrow road. It is not easy: at times it can be frustrating and at times lonely, but it is the way to discover life in all its fullness.

A guide to spirituality for the over-fifties

Beware of conforming to society's standards:
- Beware of pressures to conform to the often falling values of society.
- Look to Jesus (and Scripture) for guidance and truth.
- Be prepared to stand alone for God.
- Endurance to live Jesus' way will lead to eternal life in all its fullness – that has to be worth it!

WANTED

Volunteers to receive
riches that last:

Ever been disappointed by things that
break, rust and wear out?

Would you like riches that last for ever?

Faith (in Jesus) needed.

CHAPTER 9

True Wealth

Based on James 5:1-6, Matthew 6:25-34 and Luke 12:13-21

❡ It was my pride and joy – almost a two-seater sports car. I had first seen it in the paint shop.

'One or two stone chips,' I was told, 'because of the low mileage, we wanted to make sure that the body work was in tip top condition.'

After owning the car for a short time, rust began to peep through the paintwork: on the sills, the wings, the doors, around the lights … in fact nearly everywhere. Maybe there had been a bit more than a few stone chips!

RUST, MOULD, MOTHS, dry rot … all highlight the transience of the things of this world. The material objects that we hold so dear have a limited lifespan – in fact, I believe there is a term *manufactured obsolescence*, which means that many products are deliberately made with a limited lifespan. And of course we cannot take any of our earthly wealth with us when we die.

On what or whom do you depend?

In Matthew 6:25-34 I believe that Jesus' main emphasis is on *worry* caused by too great a dependency on the physical world and material objects. We all need to eat, drink and keep warm; hence we need a constant supply of food, water, clothes, shelter etc. There are other material things that we need on top of that, but Jesus warns us to beware of becoming too focussed on the physical at the expense of the spiritual – the things of God.

All around society today we see people getting second and even third jobs, and working longer hours. As a result they can become over-tired, worried and stressed, and extra strain is put on relationships. People are getting more and more into debt. Why? Sometimes out of necessity, but sometimes, I suspect, to buy things that are unnecessary and that they maybe don't even really want.

How we ponder on what gifts to buy different people for Christmas or birthday. Sometimes we're spoiled for choice … but often, it's because most of us have so much and need little.

We are called to be *responsible* and I believe we are given what a friend of mine referred to as *holy common sense*. However, let's be warned about the dangers of building our lives on the transient things of the physical world – making greed and materialism our gods. The dangers are further highlighted in the story of the Rich Fool.

On what does society encourage us to be dependent?

There is nothing fundamentally wrong with riches as long as we use them responsibly and generously, we do not make them our god and we make them in a way that is honest and not abusive to others.

There is the wider application of the passage in Matthew's gospel on the subject of worry. God is a God who provides, although we live in a greedy world that doesn't always share. It is so easy to waste the opportunities that today holds by worrying about what tomorrow might bring – and so lose our focus on following Jesus and the things of God.

¶ For many years I struggled to learn to swim. I was almost there, I could do a brilliant width or a length in a kind of breast stoke/doggy paddle – with one foot on the bottom of the pool. It was taking that foot off the bottom that was difficult. When I was about thirty, I started helping in a youth club: from time to time we would take them swimming. I ran out of excuses for not going and, such was my embarrassment at not being able to swim, I was finally motivated to take my foot off the bottom.

It's a bit like faith: we like to hold on to something tangible that we feel safe with, but following Jesus means letting go, allowing God to lead us and trusting him to provide – together with us playing our part, of course!

How do you feel about taking that metaphorical foot off the bottom of the pool?

A guide to spirituality for the over-fifties

To build up riches in heaven:
- Don't become too dependent on money and earthly possessions.
- Practise discernment as to the things you really need.
- Focus on following Jesus.
- Have faith – it might mean letting go of certain things.

WANTED

Patient and enduring followers:

Strength and enablement will be given.

CHAPTER 10

Patience and Faith

Based on James 5:7-20 and Mark 4:26-29

¶ Many years ago, as a young student at school, I remember being told to write a five-hundred-word essay on patience. It was part of a class punishment – we had been making too much noise whilst waiting outside the French room. I suppose, until that point, I had never thought too much about the subject of patience and waiting.

Are you a patient person?

IN VERSE 7 James highlights that we are called to demonstrate patience as we await Jesus' return: 'Be patient, then, brothers, until the Lord's coming.' I have to admit that I do struggle with patience. But the implication is that, in all things, God's timing is perfect and should not be hurried. James compares the waiting for Jesus' return with the way in which a farmer waits for his crops to grow and ripen for harvest. I couldn't help drawing a parallel with the Parable of the Growing Seed (Mark 4:26-29). The farmer has certain important tasks to perform – preparing the soil, planting, weeding etc. – but then he has to wait for God's hand to bring about growth and a harvest. Just so, during that time of waiting for Jesus' return, we are called to perform certain tasks in building the kingdom; and then await God's hand to produce growth and a harvest.

In verse 8 James speaks about us standing firm.

❡ It's funny how we are sometimes prepared to stand firm on quite trivial of things such as disputes over hedges that are too high and blocking out the light, or the preservation of an item of quite minor historical value, and yet neglect issues of real importance such as the starving millions in the world, social injustice, moral values and so on.

What do you consider to be important issues?
Would you be prepared to take a stand on some or all of them?

James is referring to God calling us to stand firm on those important issues based on his values and the teaching of Jesus. It calls for courage and boldness – being prepared to stand in isolation.

In verse 9 we are told not to grumble, not to take a negative view on life, but to be positive and constructive in our approach. As followers of Jesus, we are called to be his body – to be salt and light in the world. Let us treat even the most difficult situations as challenges and opportunities. In times of difficulty, suffering and hardship we are called to patiently persevere.

❡ 'For how many years have you been writing?' people ask me. They look very surprised at my reply, especially when I continue: 'It must have been ten … or maybe eleven years before I managed to get a book accepted for publication'.

It was a lesson in patience and perseverance but, more importantly, a time of learning and refining. God was most certainly at work in me! When the time was right, God enabled publication to take place.

In verses 13-20, 'The prayer of a righteous man is powerful and effective', James turns to prayer. It is God's intention that we should pray with faith and expectation.

❧ A few weeks ago, my family and I acquired five chickens of assorted colours and sizes. I'm sure that the man we bought them from thought we were very strange people as we told him the crazy names we had chosen for them: mine was to be Dolly Dowdeswell. We were surprised at the different personalities each of the hens seemed to possess and very soon we had bonded with them. We eagerly awaited the first egg – it was Dolly who laid it. Soon two of the others began to lay. Each day, we would make trips to the nesting box, looking in with excitement and expectation.

God wants us to be filled with that same kind of intrigue and expectation – *but much more!* – in our prayer lives. He wants us to be excited about prayer and to believe in faith that great things will happen as a result. God does answer prayers in amazing ways – not always how we would expect or in the time we would like, but his ways and timing are perfect in the eternal perspective of things.

The God who calls us to be patient in our faith is the same God who is at work in preparation for a wonderful harvest of the Kingdom.

A guide to spirituality for the over-fifties

Strive for patience and endurance:
- Ask for God's strength and enablement – it might not happen immediately.
- Respond positively to life's challenges and God's opportunities.
- Don't give up!
- Pray with faith and expectation.

WANTED
Pray'ers:

Need to be flexible and committed.

No previous training or experience required.

Answers will be given.

CHAPTER 11

Prayer

Based on James 5:13-18 and Matthew 6:5-13

¶ Several years ago, I recall being stopped in the street by a
friend. The topic of conversation got onto Church. 'I understand you're a Methodist,' she observed. I nodded. She
frowned, looking very concerned. 'When you pray in Church,
do you sit or kneel?'

What is your experience of prayer?

IF YOU FEEL comfortable kneeling to pray, that's okay; but if
you are unable to kneel or just chose not to, that's fine as well.
Let's not get too hung up on how, where and when we should
pray. Through Jesus, we have direct access to God in prayer.
God is everywhere, so it really doesn't matter where we pray:
in Church, in a quiet place at home, whilst taking the dogs out
for a walk, at the kitchen sink or some other busy place. God
is never off duty, so we can pray at any time. I'm sure that God
doesn't mind if we stand, sit, kneel, lie down, walk, run or jump
as we pray. Let's just get on and do it!

❡ Wherever we go these days, health and safety regulations dictate that everyone is aware of what to do in an emergency. We are told the location of things such as the emergency exits and fire extinguishers and, when applicable, life jackets. In our modern cars we have numerous air bags. They are tucked away in concealed locations. Generally they are never seen unless a collision occurs and then, suddenly, those potentially life-saving devices appear as if from nowhere!

Many people see prayer in that context – something that we hope we will never have to use, but it is there to fall back on if things get desperate. That's not how James sees it. He encourages us to pray when we are in trouble, pray for the sick, pray for forgiveness, pray in times of need and in good times. We should pray for each other and for ourselves. Pray about everything! Prayer should be an intrinsic ingredient of our relationship with God; sharing everything with him, including our concerns about others.

Are you good at relating to other people?
Think about some of the different kinds of relationships you have experienced in your life.

Communication is essential to any relationship. As with any dialogue there are times when we should be quiet and listen. Prayer is a two-way thing, demanding that we learn to listen to God. He speaks to us in many different ways: through Scripture, in conversations with Christian friends, through circumstances and that feeling of something being the right/wrong thing to do. He does answer prayers that are prayed in faith but beware: God sometimes says 'No' or 'Wait'.

❡ A fellow student at college was talking about being faced with a crisis in her life. She was not familiar with prayer. In desperation she said the only prayer she knew – Our Father.

The Lord's Prayer – the prayer that Jesus taught us – is a wonderful prayer, both to use as it is and also as a guide for our own prayers. We can learn so much from Jesus' example and teaching about prayer and praying.

❡ I never had any problem thinking about God being a loving, caring father – after all, that's what fathers are, isn't it? But some years ago I was talking to a teenage girl whose relationship with the father figures in her life had not been good. 'I really struggle with the image of God being our Heavenly Father,' she shared.

Even comparing God with a loving mother, grandparent or friend can fail when someone has never really experienced a close relationship of love and trust with anyone. Sadly, we live in a materialistic and, in many ways, selfish society in which abuse, neglect and family breakdown seem to be on the increase. All that can be said is that God is everything that a good parent or friend *could and should* ever be.

What can you learn about God from your experience of parents or friends?

The Lord's Prayer begins by encouraging us to relate to God both in terms of a close parent–child type of relationship and at the same time one of reverence. It focuses both on our own personal needs and concerns, as well as on the larger and even eternal perspective. The prayer recognises that God is our source of power and that his will is paramount. It is an inclusive prayer that does not use the words 'my', 'me' or 'I' once; instead it uses 'our' and 'us'.

We live in a society where the potential to communicate is greater than it has ever been thanks to email, mobile telephones, the internet, radio, TV etc. Yet, it seems to be increasingly difficult to get anyone to listen: everyone seems to be busy, pre-occupied; then there are those recorded messages that we seem to be confronted with so often at call centres. God loves to hear our prayers and he is always available. We all enjoy a good chat with a close friend or member of the family: someone with whom we don't feel that we have to put on any airs and graces, though not forgetting that any relationship demands respect and decorum. That's how it should be when we chat with God!

A guide to spirituality for the over-fifties

Be committed to prayer:
- Speak to God anywhere and at anytime.
- Pray about everything.
- Listen as well as talk.
- Use and learn from the prayer that Jesus taught us.
- Enjoy speaking with God.

WANTED

Loving people to share the love of Jesus with others:

Think the world could do with more love?

Want to be more like Jesus?

Willing to share his love with others?

The love will be supplied.

CHAPTER 12

Loved and Valued

Based on James 5:19-20, Matthew 5:43-48 and Luke 10:25-37

MY FAMILY AND I are all animal lovers. Though the experts tell us that animals do not have the ability to love, I am often astonished by the friendliness and loyalty that many pets show, not only to their owners, but often to complete strangers. Sadly, amongst the human population, such qualities often seem to be lacking. When Jesus talks about love in Matthew 5:43-48, 'If you love those who love you, what reward will you get?', his emphasis is that so often our love for others is conditional. We love those who earn our love in different ways: those who provide for us in some way, those who are kind and generous towards us, those whose looks or personalities attract us. Jesus introduces us to a new way of thinking. What about loving those who lack qualities that endear? What about loving those who have done nothing to earn our love? What about loving those who dislike, bully or abuse us? This not only requires a different way of thinking, but it also requires a divine enablement.

Have there been people in your life that you have found difficult to love?
Maybe you are struggling with such an issue at present.

❧ I recall gasping for breath, clutching my swollen nose as I headed for the safety of the corridor outside the school music room. It had been an unprovoked attack from a group of boys who had been pursuing me for some time. It came to an end when the ringleader moved away with his family a year or two later. It is only quite recently that the horrors of bullying – and the long-term damage caused by it – seem to have been realised. As I think about the way I suffered at the hands of those lads during three of the most important years of my school life, the reality of what Jesus is asking us to do in the Sermon on the Mount is driven home.

Love can be very costly. Lonely and vulnerable people can be very demanding on our time. The poor and needy can be demanding on our money and other material resources. Loving those who have mistreated us involves forgiving and forgetting, which isn't always easy. Showing Christian love for others and being there for them can be very draining on our material and emotional resources. And, at the end of the day, we should not expect anything in return. Those who we help may not show any gratitude for what we have done. We may never see or hear from them again after we have shared their difficult journey with them.

The classic parable about love in action is the Parable of the Good Samaritan. The hero of the story illustrates all these points about love: he shows love to someone he would have considered to be an enemy and it proves to be costly in a number of ways. What kind of people might be in need of our love in active, helpful ways today – victims of crime or abuse; the lonely and bereaved; the sick, frail and vulnerable; the poor?

❧ My experience as a Christian counsellor suggests to me that how we relate/have related to key people in our lives affects all the other relationships we are involved with.

Our potential to love others is dependent on our relationship with Jesus and the love that we receive from him. In his letter, John talks about the cycle of God's love only being made complete when we receive that love through Jesus and pass it on to those around us – 'but if we love one another, God lives in us and his love is made complete in us' (1 John 4:12).

Do you feel valued?

Our potential to value others is related to us feeling valued ourselves. When I think about Jesus dying on the cross for me, paying the penalty for the wrong things I have done, I feel really valued. He did the same for you! When we repent and follow the risen Jesus, then we experience his forgiveness and peace in a way that only goes to emphasise that feeling of being valued.

Matthew 5:45-48 emphasises that when we love each other in this way, then we become more like God. That likeness that was in us when we were created in his image, but damaged by sin, begins to be restored.

❦ For years, I made fun of my Dad's thinning hair. My own hair began to thin when I was about thirty. Now my own son makes fun of my lack of hair. I have promised him that some day his hair will go the same way!

It has been said that we all resemble our parents and often the characteristics that irritate us about our parents are the same characteristics that we portray in our own lives. As Christians, our sole ambition should be to grow more like our heavenly parent, demonstrated in the life and example of Jesus: 'And we, who with unveiled faces all reflect the Lord's glory, are being transformed into his likeness with ever increasing glory, which comes from the Lord, who is the Spirit.'

(2 Corinthians 3:18) This assures us that when we follow Jesus and are filled with the Holy Spirit, and as long as we allow him to, the Holy Spirit will progressively transform us more into the likeness of Jesus himself – a work that will be completed when Jesus returns (1 John 3:2).

A guide to spirituality for the over-fifties

Share Jesus' love with others:
  • Prayerfully receive his love.
  • Share it unconditionally.
  • Be prepared for there to be a cost in time and effort.
  • Draw close to Jesus and allow his Holy Spirit to progressively transform you more into his likeness.

> **WANTED**
>
> **Sinners are sought:**
>
> To receive forgiveness and be fully restored.
>
> All types of sin considered.

CHAPTER 13

Forgiven and Restored

Based on James 5:19-20 and Luke 15:11-32

❡ When accusations are made against me, sometimes I try to justify my actions. However, sometimes there is no justification – there are not even vaguely acceptable excuses. At those times I recognise that the only option open to me is to say, 'Sorry'.

THE YOUNGER SON in the Parable of the Prodigal Son reaches the point of realising the errors of his ways, and that the only way to move forwards is to put his pride behind him, return to his father and say 'Sorry'.

Talking about sin is maybe not particularly politically correct these days. James 5:19-20 highlights the destructive qualities of sin, and the resulting guilt, when it is not dealt with. Romans 3:23 says that we have all sinned. Romans 3:24 points us to Jesus as being the way to find freedom from the consequences of sin: because the living Jesus paid the penalty for our sin, by giving his life on the cross for each one of us. The Christian testimony is one of reaching that point of realisation that the only way forward is to say 'Sorry' to Jesus and allow him to cleanse, fill and transform our lives.

At what point do you say 'Sorry'?
Do you really mean it?

❦ Some people have excellent memories, some people forget. I write endless numbers of lists. Unless my wife leaves me a written note to hang out the washing – it remains in the washing machine! I think it's probably that I get very preoccupied with the things that I do. It can be all too easy to remember the things that people have done to harm or upset us. They seem to willingly come to mind during those arguments or times of one-up-manship.

The words, 'I forgive you!' are very easily said. I have to admire the honesty of those who admit that, on occasions, they really struggle to forgive. Complete forgiveness bears no grudges, makes no conditions and should be deliberately forgetful of the incident in question. We must take our example from Jesus as he hangs on the cross and forgives those responsible, and look to God for the divine enablement to put it into practice.

Do you excel at forgiving others?
What are you like at being forgiven?

The story of the lost son illustrates the wonderful forgiveness that God offers through Jesus. The kind of forgiveness that accepts us as we are, bears no grudges and is so complete that past failures to live up to God's standards will never be remembered again.

❦ I remember my mum's face as she tore off the decorative paper, to uncover two china plates with a delicate floral pattern. They were a present from my aunt and uncle. Immediately they took pride of place either side of the mantelpiece. One day, as teenagers, my brother and I had a dispute. I threw a slipper at him as he scurried out of the lounge. As soon as I had thrown it, I realised that my aim was lacking. 'Crash!' One of the plates fell over and, after balancing precariously on the edge, it fell onto the hearth and broke. It happened so quickly. If I could have undone it, I would have! If only I could have restored it to its former condition. I suspect that, even if I had meticulously glued all the individual pieces together, the joins would have still been very evident.

It is one thing to do a repair job; it is something completely different to fully restore something. The younger son in the story is quite prepared to return to a lesser role – maybe as a servant in his father's household – but no, he is fully restored to his former position, given new clothes, a ring and the fatted calf. Through faith and repentance in Jesus, we are restored fully and without blemish: entering into a parent–child relationship with God the Father, progressively being transformed by the Holy Spirit into the people that God created us to be (into the likeness of Jesus himself) and we are filled with the hope of receiving the inheritance prepared for us by God.

Those two verses in James also highlight that the response of receiving the forgiveness and restoration through Jesus is to tell others so that they too may meet with and respond to Jesus.

A guide to spirituality for the over-fifties

Know the freedom, peace and hope of being forgiven and restored:
- We've all sinned – but Jesus has paid the penalty.
- Saying 'Sorry' to Jesus is the way forward.
- God's love and acceptance is unconditional, and his forgiveness and restoration is complete.
- When you've found it, tell others.

WANTED

A positive response:

Feeling hopeless?

Does the future look bleak?

No plans for eternity?

Are you willing to follow Jesus?

Apply in prayer.

CHAPTER 14

Hope for Eternity

Based on James 5:19-20, Matthew 6:19-24 and Matthew 22:1-14

I BELIEVE THAT we all need to have hopes and dreams; surely it is an essential part of the motivation we need to live our lives – even though some may never happen. I don't know which is worse: someone with unrealistic hopes and dreams or someone with none at all. It is so sad to listen to a person who, through circumstances or illness, is finding life such a struggle that they are unable to think beyond the immediate.

What are your hopes and dreams in life?
What are your hopes and dreams for eternity?

It never ceases to amaze me when I hear about the enormous wealth of many celebrities today. We see photographs on TV and in magazines of their luxury villas and mansions across the world. Their earning capacity in a few days, or even hours, is more than many people receive in a year. Yet when serious illness or old age arrives, there comes a time when, even with all their celebrity status and wealth, their lives cannot be prolonged.

In the Sermon on the Mount, Jesus discourages investment in the material things of this world. They are so easily destroyed by things like insects, fungus and corrosion. The implication is that there are investments that last – treasures in heaven. That does not mean that we should wish our lives on earth away, dreaming only of a life to come in heaven. Once again it's all about our focus needing to be on the things of God. In Matthew 6:19-24 Jesus highlights two things. The first is that our hopes and dreams for life should be God-centred and not self-centred or materialistic. We should live a life of service, loving one another, being salt and light, witnessing for Jesus and being the body of Christ in the damaged, hurting world today. The second is that there is an eternal hope to which we should aspire. It is this hope that we are going to look at in this chapter.

℘ I recall my own wedding day with great fondness and nostalgia. It was a wonderful day, although the build up was not without its problems: only weeks before, we had to find a new venue for the reception; and then there were the wedding clothes. There were the usual dilemmas: colours, styles, co-ordination …

I have heard it said that in the parable Jesus told in Matthew 22:1-14, the wedding clothes were provided for the guests by the host. Not only would that make life so much easier, it also helps us to make more sense of the story. The wedding banquet represents heaven: the ultimate joining together of Jesus and his followers, the ultimate in relationship with God, an end to suffering and the beginning of uninterrupted blessing. The only qualification for entry is to be wearing the right clothes. Galatians 3:27 speaks about clothing ourselves in Jesus through faith in him. Ephesians 6:14 speaks about wearing the breastplate of righteousness.

Chapter 14 spoke about repentance, faith, forgiveness and following the living Jesus. This chapter is all about the application of that forgiveness, i.e. what difference being forgiven makes to our futures – now and eternally. For a moment, let us focus on our eternal futures. Jesus gave his life for us, on the cross, paying the penalty for our sin. It is only through metaphorically being clothed in Jesus, his goodness and his act of redemption that we become acceptable in God's presence and receive eternal life with him in heaven. Thereby we are saved from sin's consequences and in that lies our eternal hope. It's a difficult concept to understand; but let me use a simple illustration.

¶ I understand that an orphaned foal has poor chance of survival if it is hand fed. That young horse's best chance of life is in being adopted by another mare, who is in milk. However, horses are not generally willing to adopt another's foal. The way the experts organise it is to find a mare whose foal has died and cover the orphaned foal with the skin of the dead foal. Then, usually after a short time, the mare will accept the orphaned foal as her own. Through that acceptance the youngster has every chance of being saved.

Through being clothed in Jesus, we are accepted by God and are saved to eternal life in heaven.

Once again, I ask:
What are your hopes and dreams in life?
What are your hopes and dreams for eternity?

A guide to spirituality for the over-fifties

Live in hope, now and for eternity:
- Focus on the things of God.
- Live for others.
- Follow Jesus, accept his forgiveness and be clothed in his goodness.

WANTED

Compassionate people:

To build and restore relationships.

To work as part of a team, led by Jesus.

CHAPTER 15

Relating to Jesus and Each Other

Based on James 5:19-20 and Matthew 25:31-46

❡ Do you remember your first love? Maybe it was a romance in the playground or on the school bus. It probably didn't last long, and was probably never particularly serious, but there seems to be something quite memorable about such encounters. Perhaps you stayed together; more likely you have moved on from that first love. As folk often seem to do, maybe you hold on to memories of a relationship that seems to be almost too perfect to be real – and probably is. It could be the active imaginations of young people, a touch of the rose-tinted spectacles or even the fact that time often distorts our memories of relationships.

OF COURSE, RELATIONSHIPS are not just romantic encounters – there is a multitude of other relationships: family, friendship, colleagues at work, neighbours, those we meet on the bus or train etc.

How many different types of relationship does your day usually consist of?

❡ It never ceases to amaze me when I hear things that folk say about a work colleague at their leaving party. I recall one such occasion that was laid on for me. It was a lovely occasion, and I appreciated all that was said and done, but I wondered if people really meant what they were saying in their glowing accounts of my conduct. Situations can also distort our memories of relationships.

Maybe relationships have always been particularly hard for you because of some kind of abusive situation you have endured in the past. The reality of relationships can so often be distorted by the passing of time, changing circumstances, painful experiences and a variety of other reasons. In truth, relationships are not one of life's *easy options* – far from it! However, life could not exist without relationships; and, indeed, it would end up a very meaningless experience without them.

In an earlier chapter we looked at *love*; now we look at *relationships*. Obviously there are areas where the two topics overlap, especially when looked at from a Christian perspective. *Relationships* – the people we meet and communicate with on a day to day basis, and the way that we relate with them. Yes, as Christians our relationships should all be encompassed with love, but I believe that there are additional qualities necessary. We need to be prepared to make ourselves vulnerable enough to allow interaction to take place. We need to be flexible and generous enough in order to allow co-operation. There needs to be sufficient commitment to bring about growth and we need to have sufficient wisdom to discern behaviour appropriate to that particular relationship and act upon it.

I believe that our ability to make good relationships is very dependent on a few key relationships in our lives. The most fundamental relationship being with Jesus (and God the Father and the Holy Spirit): in him lies our primary dynamic for relating to others. Next to that are close, safe, dependable loving family or friends.

How good is your relationship with Jesus?

Let's look at our relationship with Jesus in terms of those additional characteristics. The vulnerability is the *letting go* of the things of this world that we feel safe and secure with and becoming Christ-centred rather than self-centred. The flexibility and generosity is in allowing the Holy Spirit to transform and guide our lives. The commitment is to prayer, Bible study and listening to Jesus. We need to ask God for the wisdom required in order for us to make correct decisions within that relationship.

Who is the celebrity you would most like to meet – an actor, singer, politician, member of the Royal Family? Imagine how you would feel if you received a letter from that person saying that he/she is coming to stay with you for a few days. I expect that nothing would be too much trouble: the best room, the newest bed linen and towels, the tastiest and most expensive food and drink. How then would you react to the request for help from the neighbour or work colleague whom you have always found rather abrasive or worse?

In Matthew 25:31-46 Jesus highlights the importance of relating with others – even those to whom we might not chose to relate. I picture the *good deeds* in the passage as part of a deep ongoing concern for society involving relating to others in Christ-like ways, demonstrating the qualities of vulnerability, flexibility, generosity, commitment and wisdom as well as love. Indeed, as we examine Jesus' encounters with people in the Gospels, he always seems to enter into the situation at the level of relationship – for example his meeting with Zacchaeus – rather than in a distant manner. This passage from Matthew's gospel, as well as illustrating relating to others in a Christ-like way, would also appear to confirm the fact that our ability to relate in a loving and appropriate manner to other people is directly linked to our relationship with Jesus. The good deeds in this passage are not a way of trying to earn favour/love from Jesus; instead they are a *response* to a relationship with him. It is the *evidence* of such a relationship and not the *means*.

A guide to spirituality for the over-fifties

Build good relationships:
- Think about all the different relationships you form: family, friends, neighbours, work colleagues, strangers etc.
- Prayerfully seek the necessary qualities for forming good relationships.
- Let your relationships be Christ-centred.

```
WANTED
A response to
God's Christmas gift:

The person of JESUS.
```

CHAPTER 16

Personal Response/The Future
Based on Luke 15:1-32

MOST OF US like a good party – at Christmas, New Year, birthdays, anniversaries, house warming, celebrating exam successes or promotion.

❡ I recall some years ago now, celebrating my fortieth birthday. My wife, June, had organised a surprise party at a local restaurant. Babysitters had been arranged. 'I'd like to take you out somewhere nice.' 'Just the two of us?' I mumbled.

When we arrived at the restaurant, I was surprised to see a number of folk that we knew. 'What a surprise seeing all these people here tonight,' I thought. It still hadn't clicked – not until we all sat down at the same table!

The story about a lost sheep in Luke chapter fifteen is one of a series of three – all about finding lost things/people. The story begins with a shepherd searching for his lost sheep and ends with a party when he finds it. The second story begins with a lady looking for a lost coin and ends with a party when she finds it. Similarly, the last story is about a father who is seeking a lost son and it ends with a party when the son returns home! Why all the parties? After all, some people believe that being a Christian means that we should be sullen and miserable!!

Not true!!

It's an amazing thing when someone throws a party for you because they love and appreciate you, and people come to that party because they love and appreciate you and want to show that.

- The shepherd throws a party because the sheep that was lost has been found.
- The lady throws a party because the one coin that was lost has been found.
- The father throws a party because the one son that was lost has been found.

In the same way there is rejoicing in heaven for each one of us as we return to the Father. That rejoicing is not just in heaven but also amongst God's family here on earth.

Genesis 1:27 says that God created us in his own image: to be likeminded – with a conscience; with certain creative skills; with the potential to love and be loved; to share friendship with each other – but most of all with God. We are incomplete if we are not in close relationship with God. When we turn our backs on him we are struggling like the lost sheep or the lost son. That's why there is rejoicing in heaven when someone is reunited with God – the lost is found – because he longs for us to be complete and fulfil the purpose for which we were created. Jesus' mission is to seek and save the lost.

Do you feel lost?

John's gospel is well-known for Jesus' statements beginning with the words 'I am ...' In the first half of John chapter ten there are two such verses: Jesus says, 'I am the gate for the sheep' and 'I am the good shepherd.' His first point is that the only legitimate way in is through the gate: 'Jesus answered "I am the way"' (John 14:6). The only way to be forgiven for the wrong things we have done; the only way to be set free from sin's consequences; the only way to heaven; the only way to enter into a close relationship with God the Father is through faith in Jesus. He is the gate, the only legitimate way into the Kingdom. His second point is to highlight Jesus' selfless love for us. Jesus died on the cross, paying the penalty for our sin and rose on the third day. It is because of this that he is the gate for us to enter into the Kingdom – through faith. It also illustrates the closeness of the relationship between Jesus and his followers.

> *Are there times when your faith is tested?*
> *Do you find the Christian journey a struggle sometimes?*

The Christian life *is* an ongoing journey. It can be a struggle at times and sometimes our faith and commitment are really tested. Acts 2:42-47 is an example of how we can grow spiritually. The early followers of Jesus were devoted to prayer, Bible study, breaking of bread, praising God, sharing, spending time in fellowship with other Christians and being part of a witnessing people.

A guide to spirituality for the over-fifties

Jesus' mission is to the lost – Romans 3:23 says that's all of us:
- Be sure of your commitment to Jesus.
- Be confident. Remember that when we have faith in Jesus, he is with us always (Matthew 28:20).
- Allow the Holy Spirit the freedom to work in your life, equipping you for the journey ahead – living out the Christian life of love and witness (Acts 1:8).
- Devote yourself to prayer, Bible study, breaking of bread, praising God, sharing, spending time in friendship with other Christians and being part of a witnessing people.

Appendix

Chapter 1:
Some people say that life is all about looking after number one – but it isn't really, is it?

- In Jesus' Sermon on the Mount, we are told to do to others as we would have them do to us (Matthew 7:12).
- In Matthew 16:24 Jesus says that following him involves denying self.
- In Matthew 22:37-40 Jesus tells us to love God with our hearts, souls and minds and to love each other as ourselves.
- Jesus washes his disciples' feet as an example of serving others (John 13:1-17).
- John 15:13 talks about selfless love being demonstrated by laying our lives on the line for others – exactly what Jesus did for us!

Lord Jesus,
You have taught us, by word and example, that following you is not about ourselves, but it is about doing God's will in caring for others.
Help me to learn to be less selfish.
Fill me with your love and compassion to share with others.
Teach me to look to you for guidance.
Amen.

Chapter 2:
Will I be free from problems if I become a Christian?

- In Matthew 16:24 Jesus speaks about his followers having to take up their cross: in other words, be prepared to endure hardships and suffering for the sake of the Kingdom.
- Jesus promises that, when we follow him, he will always be with us – through good times and bad (Matthew 28:20).

- As a result of persecution the early Christian Church spreads rapidly (Acts 8:1).
- God uses all things for good for those that love him (Romans 8:28).
- 1 Corinthians 10:13 gives us the wonderful promise that we will not be tempted beyond that which we are able to stand; and also that a way out will be provided.

Loving Lord Jesus,
You never said that following you would be easy, but you have promised to always be with me and that good will come from even the most traumatic experiences.
Strengthen me to cope with the hard times.
Give me endurance not to give up doing your work, even when the going gets difficult.
Help me to hold on to your promises that are all about hope and blessing.
Grant me compassion for those who suffer (give names and situations).
Amen.

Chapter 3:
How can I hear God speaking to me?

- God speaks to people in dreams, illustrated in the Christmas story (e.g. Matthew 2:12).
- When Jesus is tempted, he looks to scripture for guidance (Matthew 4:1-11).
- An angel leads Philip to minister to an Ethiopian in Acts 8:26-40.
- In Acts 12:10 God opens the city gate for Peter to go through during his escape from prison. He also opens and closes metaphorical doors and gates to guide us.
- The Holy Spirit guides Paul in Acts 16:6.

Heavenly Father,
Thank you for speaking to us in so many different ways: through
dreams and visions, the leading of the Holy Spirit, the words of
angels, reading scripture, doors opening and closing, and others.
Help me to hear and respond to what you are saying to me.
In Jesus' name. Amen.

Chapter 4:
What if I've failed in a big way, can I still have a fresh start?
There are stories of failure in the Bible e.g.

- Samson is weak in resisting temptation (Judges 16:15-17).
  God restores his strength one more time (Judges 16:23-30).
- King David does a terrible thing to Uriah the Hittite (2
  Samuel 11:1-27). After David repents, God forgives him
  and he continues to reign as king (2 Samuel 12:13).
- Johah tries to run away from God (Jonah 1:1-3). God
  redirects Jonah to where he wants him to be, and gives
  him a second chance to fulfil the task he is calling him to
  do (Jonah 1:17, 2:10 and 3:1-2).
- Peter denies Jesus (John 18:15-27). But he is forgiven and
  reinstated (John 21:15-17).

Lord Jesus,
Thank you that even when we fail in a big way, you can still forgive
us and offer us a chance to try again.
Fill me afresh with the power of your Holy Spirit.
Help me to strive to always do my best to be the person that you
would have me be, and do and say the things you would have me do
and say.
And help me to be truly repentant for the times I fail.
Grant me the ability to be an encourager to others who have failed.
Amen.

Chapter 5:
Can I earn my way to heaven through good works?

- A young man asks Jesus a similar question (Matthew 19:16-22). Jesus invites the young man to follow him.
- In John 14:6 Jesus says that he is the only way to enter into an eternal relationship with God.
- Romans 3:23-24 highlights two things: we are none of us good enough to earn our way to eternal life in heaven, but through faith in Jesus we can receive it as a gift.

Loving God,
Thank you for sending your Son Jesus to live amongst us to teach us more about you and your plan for creation; and for allowing him to die for us, paying the penalty for our sin. Thank you for raising him from the dead, and for him being alive today transforming the lives of those who follow him in faith. Help my response to Jesus, and for what he has done, be a positive one.
In his name I pray. Amen.

Chapter 6:
What can I do about those things that I wish I'd never said?

- Things can't be unsaid; sometimes they can't be undone either. Judas tries to undo his betrayal of Jesus – but cannot (Matthew 27:3-5).
- Hence 1 John 1:9 is a great comfort, promising forgiveness to those who ask for it in repentance and faith (in Jesus).

Lord Jesus,
Thank you for forgiving those who follow you and repent in faith. Forgive me for those careless and hurtful words which cannot be unsaid (name situations).

Forgive me for those actions that were unkind and unnecessary, which maybe cannot be undone (name situations).
Help me to resist temptation in the future; and to only use words and actions that are helpful and loving.
Have your healing touch upon those who have been hurt by careless and spiteful words and actions.
Amen.

Chapter 7:
What is wisdom?

- Solomon asks God for wisdom in 1 Kings 3:1-15.
- Hosea 14:9 highlights that true wisdom comes from God.
- Jesus tells a parable about a wise and foolish builder. He compares the wise one with someone who hears his teaching and puts it into practice (Matthew 7:24-27).

  Father God,
  Your wisdom is the true wisdom.
  Help me to discern what is of you and what is not.
  Help me to put the teaching of Jesus into practice in my life.
  Help me to be wise in all the choices and decisions that I make.
  In his name I pray. Amen.

Chapter 8:
What's wrong with wanting to be popular?
- In Matthew 4:1-11 the devil tries to tempt Jesus to win popularity by doing things with a wrong motive. Jesus refuses.
- Jesus criticises the hypocrites for praying in such a way to win themselves public admiration (Matthew 6:5).

Gracious Heavenly Father,
Help me not to strive for popularity at the expense of doing
what is right – and doing it for the right reason and with the
right motives.
Help me to turn away from things like greed, pride and jealousy.
Grant me humility I pray.
In Jesus' name. Amen.

Chapter 9:
Isn't it natural to worry about the future?

- In Matthew 8:20 Jesus highlights the importance of not becoming too dependent on material possessions and security, but to learn to trust God's provision more. However, that doesn't rule out responsibility or common sense. There is a balacnce that we need to prayerfully seek.
- In Luke 10:38-42 Jesus commends Mary for her priorities.
- Look more closely at the parable Jesus tells about a rich farmer who unwisely places his dependency completely on transient material things rather than the promises of God (Luke 12:13-21).

Father in heaven,
Thank you for all your wonderful promises in the Bible; and
that your promises never fail.
Help me not to become too dependent and focused on material
things that are so transient; but instead, to place my hope and
security primarily in Jesus and heavenly treasure.
But, at the same time, help me not to waste the opportunities to
serve you while I'm here on earth.
In Jesus' name. Amen.

Chapter 10:
Why does God sometimes make us wait for things?

- The Bible advocates patience and perseverance in awaiting God's perfect timing. His gifts are worth waiting for (see Psalm 37:7 and Acts 1:4).

  Generous Heavenly Father,
  Thank you that you give good gifts to us and that your timing
  is perfect.
  Help me to be patient and persevering as I wait for answers
  to prayer.
  (Name some of the good gifts God gives and thank him.)
  (Pray for own needs and the needs of others.)
  In Jesus' name. Amen.

Chapter 11:
How should I pray?

- Jeremiah 29:12 tells us that when we pray God listens – I believe he does that, even when we don't get it quite right.
- There is a lot of teaching in the Bible about prayer; but one of the most important verses is 1 Thessalonians 5:17, which tells us not to allow our hang-ups about praying to prevent us from spending time doing it!

  Loving God,
  Thank you that you love to listen to our prayers.
  Help me to spend time reading the Bible to find out more about
  prayer.
  In the meantime, help me not to get so preoccupied with how to
  pray that I allow it to put me off spending time in prayer.
  In Jesus' name. Amen.

Chapter 12:
Is it okay to seek revenge?

- In Matthew 5:39 Jesus speaks about turning the other cheek.
- A few verses later, Jesus tells us to pray for our enemies (Matthew 5:44).
- After Jesus has spent time teaching about prayer he tells us that we should forgive others (Matthew 6:14-15).

Lord Jesus,
Thank you that you not only offer us forgiveness, but you are our example.
Help me to forgive those who hurt, upset or offend me.
Give me a love for those who I find difficult to befriend.
Let there be more love and care in the world generally, today.
Amen.

Chapter 13:
I'm not good enough to go to church – am I?

- In Matthew 9:12 Jesus says that it is the sick who need a doctor. In other words his mission was and is for people who are imperfect.
- In Luke 19:10 Jesus refers to his mission being aimed at those who are lost.
- Romans 3:23 says quite clearly that we are all imperfect because we have all fallen short of God's standards – but Jesus' mission is for imperfect people!

Living Lord Jesus,
Thank you that your mission is for imperfect people like me.
Thank you that you loved me so much that you died on the cross, paying the penalty for my sin, and rose again.
Come into my life, forgive me for the things that I have done

wrong, restore my relationship with God and begin to cleanse
and transform me with your Holy Spirit.
Empower me to help in your ministry to the lost.
Amen.

Chapter 14:
What is eternal life?

- We are made in the image of God (Genesis 1:27) – God is eternal. The Bible talks a lot about our eternal potential and how we approach it.
- John 17:3 reveals that the way to find eternal life in all its fullness is through entering into a relationship with God the Father through repentantly turning away from living a sinful lifestyle to following Jesus.

Eternal God,
Thank you that you created me in your likeness with the
potential to enter into an eternal relationship with you.
Thank you that Jesus made that relationship possible.
Help me to turn away from a sinful lifestyle and follow Jesus.
In his name I pray. Amen.

Chapter 15:
I like my own company, what's wrong with that?

- We are made in God's image to relate with him and each other (Genesis 1:27).
- In Genesis 2:18 God says that it is not good for Adam to be alone.

Father God,
Thank you that you want to be my friend.
Help me with all the different types of relationships that I enter

*into: family, neighbours, friendships, work colleagues – so
different, and not always easy.
I pray for your special healing touch on relationships in general
in the world today.*
(Pray for national and international unrest caused by
breakdown of relationships.)
In Jesus' name. Amen.

Chapter 16:
Does God really have a plan for my life?

• Jeremiah 29:11 confirms that God has a really good plan
  for each one of us – if we are willing to be part of it.

*Loving Heavenly Father,
Thank you that you have a plan for my life which involves
hope and blessing.
Help me to walk in that plan.
Give me the courage, perseverance, commitment and faith to
keep my eyes fixed on Jesus and follow him all my life.
Fill me afresh with the Holy Spirit and help me to understand
and live by your word, to be constantly in prayer and fellowship
with you and other Christians.
Help me to be more like Jesus as I strive to live the Christian life
of love and witness.
In Jesus' name. Amen.*